Flower Pots

Cindy Lammon

Flower

Cindy Lammon

Pots

Martingale®
& COMPANY

Flower Pots
© 2009 by Cindy Lammon

That Patchwork Place® is an imprint
of Martingale & Company®.

Martingale & Company
20205 144th Ave. NE
Woodinville, WA 98072-8478 USA
www.martingale-pub.com

Printed in China
14 13 12 11 10 09   8 7 6 5 4 3 2 1

Library of Congress Cataloging-in-Publication Data
Library of Congress Control Number: 2009020328

ISBN: 978-1-56477-945-8

Mission Statement

Dedicated to providing quality products and service to inspire creativity.

Credits

President & CEO: Tom Wierzbicki
Editor in Chief: Mary V. Green
Managing Editor: Tina Cook
Developmental Editor: Karen Costello Soltys
Technical Editor: Ellen Pahl
Copy Editor: Marcy Heffernan
Design Director: Stan Green
Production Manager: Regina Girard
Illustrator: Laurel Strand
Cover & Text Designer: Adrienne Smitke
Photographer: Brent Kane

Table of Contents

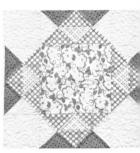

Container gardening is quite the rage these days for many reasons. Even a complete novice can create a beautiful garden using pots and seeds or purchased plants. Potted plants can be used in even the smallest of spaces and moved around to suit your mood. You can be wildly creative in your choice of containers and plants, and with the instant gratification of potted plants, you have a garden in no time!

The quilt in this book was inspired by the creativity and variety that container gardening offers. You'll make a variety of blocks, and you'll find them amazingly easy! The best thing about it—no digging in the dirt! I hope you enjoy making your Flower Pot Quilt!

Quiltmaking Basics

On the following pages, I've included the basic techniques used to make this quilt. Read through these basics, and you'll be ready to create your own Flower Pot Quilt!

Rotary Cutting

For rotary cutting, you will need a rotary cutter, a self-healing mat that is at least 24" in one direction, and an acrylic ruler that is at least 24" long. A second smaller ruler is helpful for squaring up your fabric, and it will also come in handy for trimming fabric edges. The instructions that follow are for right-handed quilters. Reverse the process if you are left-handed.

1. Square up your fabric by aligning a small square ruler along the folded edge. Place a larger 24" ruler to the left of the small ruler, butting it up to the small ruler as shown.

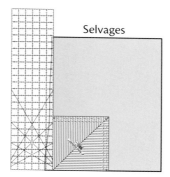

Selvages

2. Remove the small ruler and cut along the right edge of the large ruler.

3. To cut strips, position the large ruler so the desired measurement is aligned with the newly cut edge of the fabric.

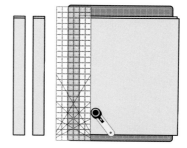

4. Once you've cut your strips, they can be crosscut into squares or rectangles. Place the strip horizontally on the cutting mat. Trim off the selvages and square up the end. Align the proper measurement on the ruler with the newly cut edge of the fabric. Cut the strip into the desired number of squares or rectangles.

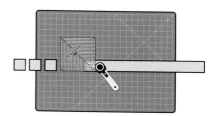

Machine Piecing

The Flower Pot quilt pattern is based on sewing with an accurate ¼" seam allowance. You can save yourself a lot of frustration by taking the time now to make sure that your ¼" seam allowance is exact.

Here's a simple test to check for an accurate ¼" seam allowance. Cut three strips 1½" x 3". Sew them together along the long edges. Press the seam allowances to one side. The resulting piece should measure 3½" across. If your piece does not measure 3½", make the necessary adjustments and try again.

3½"

Pressing

Most seam allowances in quilting are pressed to one side. After a seam is sewn, place the piece on the ironing board, and press the seam flat from the wrong side. Open the piece and press the seam allowances in the desired direction from the right side, with the edge of the iron along the seam line. Hold the iron in place; too much movement can cause distortion. Pressing from the right side in this manner prevents tucks along the seam line.

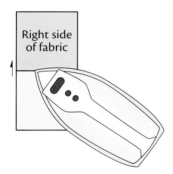

Right side of fabric

Pressing directions are included in the instructions for making the blocks. This will help with the construction of the blocks by allowing the opposing seams to "nest" for easier and accurate matching.

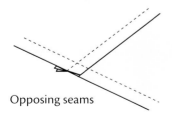

Opposing seams

Seam allowances can also be pressed open. I like to press them open to reduce bulk when there will be multiple seams coming together.

Folded Triangles

This method of sewing triangles onto the corners of other shapes eliminates the need for cutting oddly shaped pieces and dealing with bias edges.

1. Use a sharp pencil to draw a diagonal line on the wrong side of the small squares cut for your block.

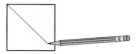

2. With right sides together, place a marked square on the corner of a larger base piece, making sure the orientation of the drawn line is correct. Sew directly on the line.

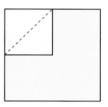

3. Press the seam as it was sewn, and then fold the square along the seam and press again. The edges of the folded square should match those of the base square or rectangle. Trim the two bottom layers leaving a ¼" seam allowance.

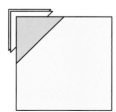

Adding Borders

Cut and piece your border strips as directed in the project instructions. They will be several inches longer than required. Use the quilt center as a guide to determine the length needed and cut the two opposite borders to that length. You can either measure across your quilt center or simply lay two border strips across the quilt center and trim them even with the raw edges of the quilt. Sew the borders on, easing the border or quilt where necessary.

Layering and Basting

Piece your backing fabric so that you have a backing that is about 4" wider and longer than the quilt top. Layer the backing, the batting, and the quilt top and secure by either thread basting (for hand quilting) or safety pins basting (for machine quilting).

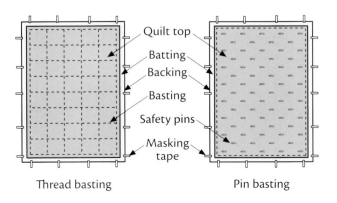

Quilting

Either hand quilting or machine quilting will work beautifully on the quilt in this book. Choose a variety of motifs, keeping the density of the quilting fairly even. Quilting the background of the appliqué designs will make them pop.

Binding

The binding for this quilt was cut on the bias, since I like the look of the striped fabric cut diagonally. The binding can also be cut cross grain (selvage to selvage) for a different look, or if you choose not to use a striped fabric. The application of the binding is the same for straight grain and bias strips.

1. To cut bias strips, open the fabric to one layer. Position your 24" ruler on the fabric, placing the 45° line on the selvage edge of the fabric. Cut along the edge of the ruler to establish the 45° angle. From the newly cut edge, cut as many 2½" strips as required. Trim the ends of the strips square.

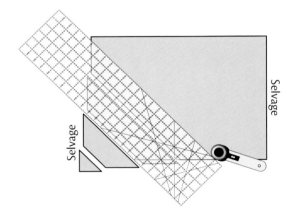

2. Place the ends of two strips right sides together at right angles. Draw a diagonal line as shown and sew on the line. Add the remaining strips in the same manner. Trim the seam allowances to ¼" and press them open.

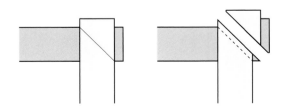

3. Fold the strip in half lengthwise, wrong sides together, and press.

4. Place the raw edge of the binding strip even with the raw edge of the quilt. Sew the binding to the quilt using a walking foot and a ¼" seam allowance, leaving about 10" free at the starting end. Sew to the first corner, stopping ¼" from the corner and backstitch.

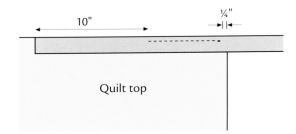

5. To miter the corner, remove the quilt from the machine. Fold the binding up so that the fold is at a 45° angle with the corner of the quilt and the raw edges are aligned with the second side of the quilt.

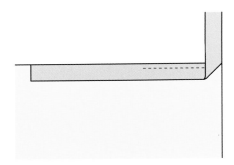

6. Fold the binding back down, aligning the fold with the top raw edge of the quilt. Align the raw edges of the binding with the raw edge of the next side of the quilt. Begin stitching at the fold and continue around the quilt, mitering each corner as you come to it.

7. Stop sewing about 10" from the starting tail. Place the quilt on a flat surface and overlap the two ends of the binding strips. Trim the overlap to a size equal to the original cut width of the binding, 2½" in this case.

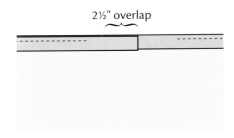

2½" overlap

8. Place the beginning and ending strips right sides together at right angles. Draw a diagonal line as you did in step 2. Pin and stitch on the line.

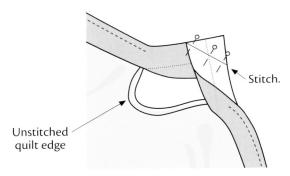

Stitch.

Unstitched quilt edge

9. Check the binding to be sure it fits correctly. Trim the seam allowances to ¼" and finger-press them open. Refold the binding, pin it in place, and finish stitching it to the quilt.

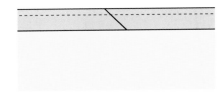

10. Fold the binding over the edge of the quilt to the back. Blind stitch the binding to the back using a thread color that matches the binding. Miters will form at the corners.

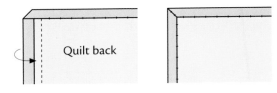

Quilt back

Appliqué Techniques

The appliqué in this quilt is very simple and can be done by machine. I used the needle-turn technique with freezer paper to hand appliqué my quilt, but feel free to use your favorite method.

Hand Appliqué

1. Trace the appliqué shape onto the dull side of freezer paper. Cut out the shape directly on the drawn line. You'll need one freezer-paper template for each appliqué piece.

2. Press the waxy side of the freezer paper to the wrong side of your fabric with a dry iron.

3. Cut out each shape, adding a scant ¼" seam allowance.

4. Pin the piece in place on the background. Appliqué using an invisible appliqué stitch, turning the seam allowance under with your needle as you go. Refer to "Invisible Appliqué Stitch" on page 13 for additional details.

5. Remove the freezer-paper templates by carefully cutting a slit in the background on the wrong side. Be careful to cut only the background fabric and not through the freezer paper. Cut out the background fabric, leaving a ¼" seam allowance around the piece. Gently tug on the freezer paper to loosen and remove it.

Machine Appliqué

1. Trace the appliqué shape onto paper-backed fusible web. Cut out the shape about ¼" from the drawn line.

2. Fuse the shape to the wrong side of the appliqué fabric, following the manufacturer's instructions. Cut the shape out on the drawn line.

3. Remove the paper backing and fuse the appliqué piece to the background.

4. Machine stitch the edges using your preferred machine stitch. See "Machine Blanket Stitch" on page 13 for details on that stitch.

Invisible Appliqué Stitch

Use a fine thread (I prefer silk) that matches the color of the appliqué shape and a fine straw needle or Sharp.

1. Use your needle to turn the edge under where you want to start sewing. The freezer paper on the wrong side prevents you from turning under too much seam allowance and provides a guide for the edge. Hold the seam allowance in place with your non-sewing hand.

2. Bring your needle up from the back, through the background, and through the fold on the edge of the appliqué piece. Take your needle back down into the background only, next to where it came up through the fold of the appliqué. Bring the needle back up about 1/16" from the previous stitch through the background and through the fold on the edge of the appliqué.

3. Continue stitching along the piece, turning under the seam allowance with the needle as you go and holding it under with your non-sewing hand. You do not need to turn under edges that will be overlapped by another piece. The raw edge will be covered by the next piece.

Machine Blanket Stitch

Use 50-weight cotton thread in a color that matches your appliqué piece. Set your machine for a blanket stitch and adjust both the width and the length to about 1/8". Stitch along the edge of the appliqué, keeping the straight stitch on the background and as close to the appliqué piece as possible. For curves and points, stop with the needle down in the background and pivot.

For an old-fashioned look, you can use black thread. Use a contrasting color if you want the stitching to be more prominent.

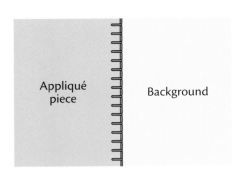

Appliqué piece   Background

14

Flower Pots

Pieced and appliquéd by Cindy Lammon. Quilted by Wanda Salzman.
Finished quilt: 57½" x 74½"

The materials listed below are sufficient to make the quilt shown. Cutting, piecing, and appliqué instructions for each block are provided on the following pages, along with a close-up photograph of each individual block.

Materials

All yardages are based on 42"-wide fabric. Fat quarters measure 18" x 21". Fat eighths measure 9" x 21".

1¾ yards *total* of assorted cream tone-on-tone fabrics for blocks and filler pieces

1⅓ yards of yellow floral for blocks, filler strips, and outer border*

1⅓ yards of striped fabric for blocks, filler strip, and binding

5 fat quarters of assorted green prints and checked fabrics for blocks **or** 1¼ yards *total*

4 fat quarters of assorted cream prints and yellow prints for blocks **or** 1 yard *total*

¾ yard of blue checked fabric for blocks and inner border

3 fat quarters of assorted medium blue prints for blocks **or** ¾ yard *total*

½ yard of dark blue print for blocks

⅓ yard of cream print for filler strips

2 fat eighths of assorted light blue prints for blocks **or** ¼ yard *total*

3¾ yards of backing fabric

62" x 79" piece of batting

Use the yellow floral as one of the yellow prints in the cutting for the blocks.

Block 1: Flower Pot

Finished size: 12" x 12"

Cutting for 7 Blocks

From *each of 7* assorted cream prints and yellow prints, cut:*

1 square, 6½" x 6½" (7 total)

1 square, 4¼" x 4¼"; cut into quarters diagonally to make 4 quarter-square triangles (28 total)

From *each of 2* assorted medium blue prints and the dark blue print, cut:

3 squares, 4¼" x 4¼"; cut into quarters diagonally to make 12 quarter-square triangles (36 total)

From *each of 3* assorted light blue prints, cut:

2 squares, 4¼" x 4¼"; cut into quarters diagonally to make 8 quarter-square triangles (24 total)

From *each of 7* assorted cream tone-on-tone fabrics, cut:*

2 squares, 4¼" x 4¼"; cut into quarters diagonally to make 8 quarter-square triangles (56 total)

4 squares, 3½" x 3½" (28 total)

From *each of 4* assorted green prints, cut:

3 squares, 4¼" x 4¼"; cut into quarters diagonally to make 12 quarter-square triangles (48 total)

From *each of 4* different assorted green prints, cut:*

2 squares, 4¼" x 4¼"; cut into quarters diagonally to make 8 quarter-square triangles (32 total)

*It's okay if you don't have enough different fabrics; simply repeat some of the fabrics in different combinations in the blocks.

Making the Block

1. Select a set of 12 matching medium or dark blue print quarter-square triangles and 4 matching cream print or yellow print quarter-square triangles for one block. Sew one blue triangle to a cream triangle along the long edge; press. Make four.

Make 4.

2. Sew a matching blue print quarter-square triangle to the unit from step 1 as shown. Select a set of eight matching light blue print quarter-square triangles. Sew one triangle to the opposite side of the unit; press. Make four.

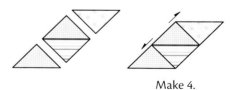

Make 4.

3. Select a set of eight matching cream tone-on-tone quarter-square triangles. Sew a blue print triangle from step 1 to a cream triangle along the short edge as shown; press. Make four.

Make 4.

4. Sew a light blue print triangle from step 2 to a cream tone-on-tone triangle as shown; press. Make four.

Make 4.

5. Sew the units from steps 3 and 4 to the unit from step 2; press. Make four.

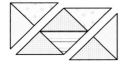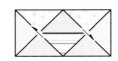

Make 4.

6. Sew 2 of the units from step 5 to opposite sides of a cream print or yellow print 6½" square; press.

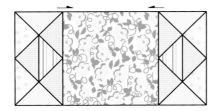

7. Sew a matching cream tone-on-tone 3½" square to opposite ends of the remaining two units from step 5; press.

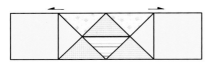

Make 2.

8. Sew the units from steps 6 and 7 together to complete the block; press. Make three blue Flower Pot blocks.

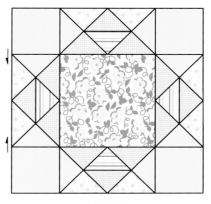

Make 3.

9. Repeat steps 1–8, replacing the blue quarter-square triangles with green triangles to make two green Flower Pot blocks.

10. Repeat steps 1–7 replacing the blue quarter-square triangles with green triangles and make two more green Flower Pot blocks, but do not sew the bottom row on yet. Leave the bottom row unattached for now.

Make 4.
Leave bottom row
unattached on 2 blocks.

Block 2: Blooming Button Flower

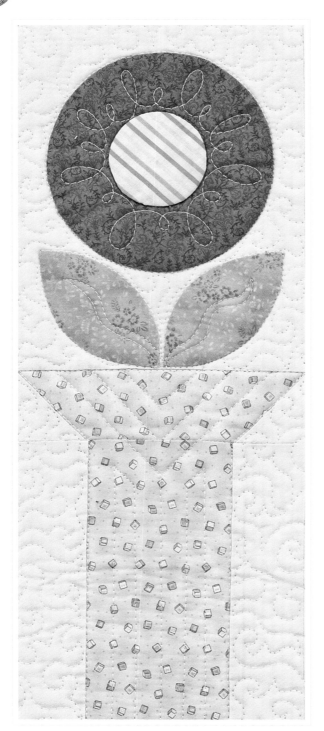

Finished size: 6" x 15"

Cutting for 4 Blocks

Template patterns for appliqués A, B, and C are on page 30.

From *each of 4* assorted cream tone-on-tone fabrics, cut:
1 rectangle, 6½" x 8" (4 total)
2 rectangles, 2" x 6½" (8 total)
2 squares, 2" x 2" (8 total)

From *each of 4* assorted blue or green prints, cut:
1 rectangle, 3½" x 6½" (4 total)
1 rectangle, 2" x 6½" (4 total)

From *each of 4* assorted green prints, cut:
2 leaves using template A (8 total)

From the assorted blue prints, *cut a total of:*
4 circles using template B

From the assorted yellow prints and the striped fabric, *cut a total of:*
4 circles using template C

Making the Block

1. Sew a cream tone-on-tone 2" x 6½" rectangle to each long side of a blue or green 3½" x 6½" rectangle; press.

2. Referring to "Folded Triangles" on page 9, use your preferred marker and a ruler to draw a line from corner to corner on the wrong side of two cream tone-on-tone 2" squares.

3. With right sides together, place a marked square on each end of a matching blue or green 2" x 6½" rectangle, noting the orientation of the drawn line. Sew on the drawn line; press. Trim the excess fabric leaving a ¼" seam allowance.

4. Sew the unit from step 3 to the unit from step 1. Sew the cream 6½" x 8" rectangle to the top; press.

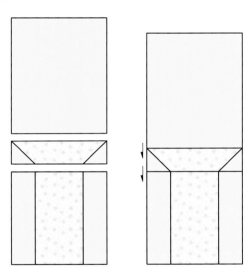

5. Referring to "Appliqué Techniques" on page 12, appliqué the leaves (A), placing one point at the center along the seam line and the second point ¾" in from the side raw edge and 2½" up from the seam line as shown. Appliqué the large blue circle (B), centering it from side to side and placing it ⅞" down from the top raw edge. Appliqué the yellow circle (C) in the center of the blue circle. Make four Blooming Button Flower blocks.

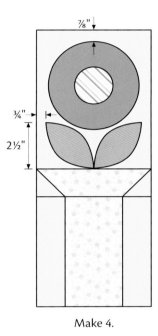

Make 4.

Block 3: Basket Bouquet

Finished size: 6" x 6"

Cutting for 5 Blocks

From *each of 5* assorted medium and dark blue prints, cut:*

2 squares, 2" x 2" (10 total)

1 square, 2⅜" x 2⅜"; cut in half diagonally to make 2 half-square triangles (10 total)

From *each of 5* assorted yellow prints, cut:*

2 squares, 2" x 2" (10 total)

From *each of 5* assorted green prints, cut:

4 squares, 2" x 2" (20 total)

From *each of 3* assorted cream tone-on-tone fabrics and 2 cream prints, cut:

4 rectangles, 2" x 3½" (20 total)

1 square, 3⅞" x 3⅞"; cut in half diagonally to make 2 half-square triangles (10 total; 5 are extra.)

1 square, 2" x 2" (5 total)

It's okay if you don't have enough different fabrics; simply repeat some of the fabrics in different combinations in the blocks.

Making the Block

1. Sew a yellow 2" square to a blue 2" square; press. Repeat with matching squares to make a second row. Sew the rows together to make a four-patch unit; press.

2. Referring to "Folded Triangles" on page 9, use your preferred marker and a ruler to draw a line from corner to corner on the wrong side of four 2" green squares.

20

3. With right sides together, place a marked green square on a cream 2" x 3½" rectangle as shown. Sew on the drawn line; press. Trim the excess fabric leaving a ¼" seam allowance. Repeat with a second marked green square on the opposite end, noting the orientation of the marked line. Make two of these flying-geese units.

4. Sew a cream 2" square to one flying-geese unit from step 3; press. Sew the second flying-geese unit to the four-patch unit from step 1; press. Sew these rows together; press.

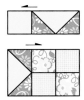

5. Sew a blue 2⅜" half-square triangle to a cream 2" x 3½" rectangle, noting the orientation of the triangle; press. Repeat, making the second unit a mirror image of the first.

6. Sew the units from step 5 to the unit from step 4; press. Center and sew the cream 3⅞" triangle to the unit; press. Make five Basket Bouquet blocks.

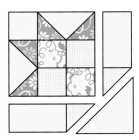 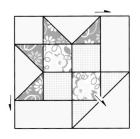

Make 5.

Block 4: Sprouting Pot

Finished size: 9" x 8"

Cutting for 3 Blocks

Patterns for appliqués C, D, E, and F are on pages 30 and 31.

From *one* cream tone-on-tone fabric, cut:
3 rectangles, 6½" x 8½"

From *one* green print, cut:
3 pots using template D

From *each of 3* assorted green prints, cut:
2 leaves using template E (6 total)

From the dark blue print, cut:
3 circles using template F

From *each of 3* assorted cream prints, cut:
1 circle using template C (3 total)

From the blue checked fabric, cut:
2 strips, 2" x 42"; cut into 6 rectangles, 2" x 8½"

Making the Block

1. Referring to "Appliqué Techniques" on page 12, appliqué the pot (D) to the cream 6½" x 8½" background. Place the bottom raw edge of the pot even with the 6½" raw edge of the background, centering it from side to side. Appliqué the sides and top of the pot; the bottom edge will be finished in the seam allowance.

2. Appliqué the leaves (E), placing one point at the center of the top edge of the pot (the center is 2½" from either side) and the second point ⅝" in from the side raw edge and 1⅝" up from the top edge of the pot. Refer to the placement diagram below.

3. Appliqué a dark blue circle (F), centering it from side to side and placing it ½" down from the top raw edge of the background. Appliqué a cream print circle (C) in the center of the blue circle.

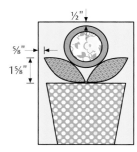

4. Sew a blue checked 2" x 8½" rectangle to each side of the block; press. Make three Sprouting Pot blocks.

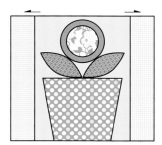

Make 3.

Finished size: 12" x 12"

Cutting for 1 Block

From *one* cream print, cut:

1 square, 2½" x 2½"; cut in half diagonally to make 2 half-square triangles

1 square, 4½" x 4½"; cut into quarters diagonally to make 4 quarter-square triangles (2 are extra)

1 square, 2⅛" x 2⅛"

1 square, 4⅛" x 4⅛"; cut in half diagonally to make 2 half-square triangles

2 rectangles, 2⅛" x 5⅜"

From the dark blue print, cut:

2 squares, 2½" x 2½"; cut in half diagonally to make 4 half-square triangles

From *one* cream tone-on-tone fabric, cut:*

1 square, 4⅛" x 4⅛"; cut in half diagonally to make 2 half-square triangles (1 is extra)

From *one* green print, cut:

2 squares, 4⅛" x 4⅛"; cut each square in half diagonally to make 4 half-square triangles (1 is extra)

1 square, 2½" x 2½"; cut in half diagonally to make 2 half-square triangles

From *a second* green print, cut:

2 squares, 8" x 8"; cut each square in half diagonally to make 4 half-square triangles**

*You can use a yellow print for the center of your basket if you prefer.

**These triangles are cut oversized; you will trim them when the block is completed.

Making the Block

1. Sew a cream print 2½" half-square triangle to a dark blue 2½" half-square triangle along the long edge; press. Make two.

Make 2.

2. Sew a dark blue 2½" half-square triangle to a cream print 4½" quarter-square triangle as shown. Repeat to make a second unit that is a mirror image of the first; press.

3. Sew the units from steps 1 and 2 together; press. Sew a cream print 2⅛" square to one unit as shown; press.

4. Sew the unit from step 3 *without* the square to a cream print 4⅛" half-square triangle; press. Sew the unit *with* the square to the adjacent side; press.

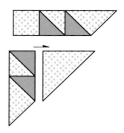 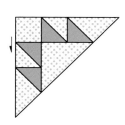

5. Sew the green 4⅛" half-square triangle to a cream tone-on-tone 4⅛" half-square triangle along the long edge; press. Sew a green 4⅛" half-square triangle to the remaining two sides of the cream triangle; press.

6. Sew the unit from step 5 to the unit from step 4; press.

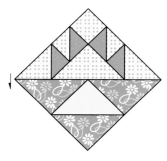

7. Sew the green 2½" half-square triangle to the cream print 2⅛" x 5⅜" rectangle as shown. Repeat to make a second unit that is a mirror image of the first; press.

8. Sew the units from step 7 to the unit from step 6; press. Center and sew a cream print 4⅛" half-square triangle to the unit; press.

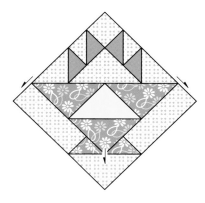

9. Center and sew green 8" half-square triangles to two opposite sides of the unit from step 8; press. Trim the corners of the triangle even with the block as shown. Sew the remaining green half-square triangles to the remaining sides of the unit; press.

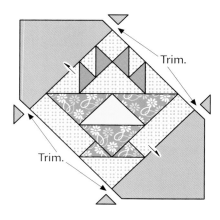

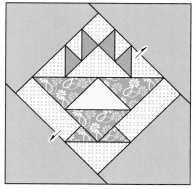

10. Trim the block to 12½" x 12½", making sure to keep the basket centered in the block. Make one Basket of Blooms block.

Block 6: Birds in My Garden

Finished size: 6" x 33"

Cutting for 1 Block

From *one* cream tone-on-tone fabric, cut:

14 squares, 3½" x 3½"
32 squares, 2" x 2"

From the assorted green and blue prints and the striped fabric, cut *a total of*:

7 rectangles, 3½" x 6½"
16 rectangles, 2" x 3½"

Making the Block

1. Referring to "Folded Triangles" on page 9, use your preferred marker and a ruler to draw a line from corner to corner on the wrong side of the cream tone-on-tone 3½" squares.

2. Place a marked square, right sides together, on an assorted blue or green print or striped 3½" x 6½" rectangle. Sew on the drawn line; press. Trim the excess fabric, leaving a ¼" seam allowance. Repeat with a second marked square on the opposite end, noting the orientation of the marked line. Make seven of these flying-geese units.

Make 7.

3. Repeat steps 1 and 2 using the cream tone-on-tone 2" squares with the assorted blue or green 2" x 3½" rectangles. Make 16 of these smaller flying-geese units.

4. Sew the units from step 3 together in pairs along the 2" edge; press the seam allowances open.

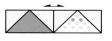

Make 8.

5. Alternate the small and large flying-geese units and sew them together in a row, beginning and ending with a small flying-geese unit; press the seam allowances open. Make one Birds in My Garden block.

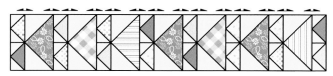

Make 1.

Block 7: Pocket Full of Posies

Finished size: 9" x 21"

Cutting for 1 Block

Patterns for appliqués G, H, and I are on page 31.

From *each of 2* cream tone-on-tone fabrics and one assorted cream print, cut:

1 rectangle, 6½" x 7½" (3 total)

From *one* cream tone-on-tone fabric, cut:

1 rectangle, 3½" x 21½"

From *each of 3* assorted blue and green prints and the striped fabric, cut:

4 flower petals using template G (12 total)

From the dark blue print, cut:

3 circles using template H

From *each of 3* green prints, cut:

2 leaves using template I (6 total)

Making the Block

1. Referring to "Appliqué Techniques" on page 12 and centering the flower, appliqué the petals (G) to the background 6½" x 7½" rectangle. Appliqué the dark blue circle (H) in the center. Make three.

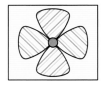

Make 3.

2. Measure 7¼" from the left raw edge of the cream 3½" x 21½" background rectangle and make a crease. Make a second crease 7" from the first; this will be 7¼" from the right raw edge. Appliqué three sets of leaves (I) using your creases as a guide for placement and centering the leaves within the 3½" x 7" rectangles. Be sure to allow ¼" on each end for the seam allowances.

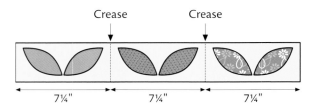

3. Sew the three flower units together along the 6½" edge. Sew the unit from step 2 to the bottom edge. Make one Pocket Full of Posies block.

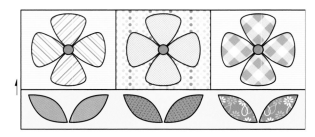

Make 1.

Assembling the Quilt

Now that all of your blocks are complete, it's time to cut the sashing and borders and assemble the quilt top.

Cutting

From the yellow floral, cut:

1 strip, 3½" x 42"; cut into:
    1 rectangle, 3½" x 12½"
    1 rectangle, 3½" x 15½"
7 strips, 5½" x 42"

From a cream tone-on-tone fabric, cut:

2 rectangles, 2" x 6½"
1 strip, 3½" x 42"; cut into:
    1 rectangle, 3½" x 6½"
    2 squares, 3½" x 3½"
    1 rectangle, 3½" x 21½"

From the striped fabric, cut:

1 rectangle, 3½" x 33½"
2½"-wide bias strips to total 275"

From the cream print for filler strips, cut:

1 strip, 5" x 42"; cut into 4 rectangles, 5" x 8½"
1 strip, 3½" x 42"; cut into:
    1 rectangle, 3½" x 12½"
    2 squares, 3½" x 3½"

From the blue checked fabric, cut:

6 strips, 1½" x 42"

Assembling Row 1

1. Referring to the row 1 diagram above right, sew a blue Flower Pot block, a green Flower Pot block, and a yellow floral 3½" x 12½" rectangle together; press. Sew the unattached row of a second green Flower Pot block to a yellow floral 3½" x 15½" rectangle along the short edge; press. Sew these two units together; press.

2. Sew three Blooming Button Flower blocks together along the long edges; press. Sew this unit to the Flower Pot unit from step 1; press.

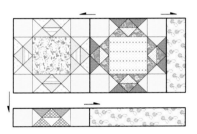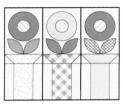

Row 1

Assembling Row 2

1. Sew the five Basket Bouquet blocks together in a row. Sew a cream tone-on-tone 2" x 6½" rectangle to each end of the row; press.

2. Sew the striped 3½" x 33½" rectangle to the bottom of the basket row; press.

3. Sew the lower section of the Flower Pot block from row 1 to the left edge; press.

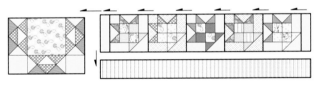

Row 2

Assembling Row 3

Alternate the three Sprouting Pot blocks with the four cream print 5" x 8½" rectangles and sew them together in a row; press.

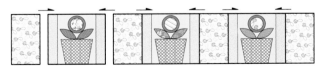

Row 3

Assembling Row 4

1. Referring to the Row 4 diagram, sew a cream tone-on-tone 3½" x 6½" rectangle to the left side of a cream print 3½" square; sew a cream tone-on-tone 3½" square to the right side; press. Sew this unit to the bottom of the Basket of Blooms block; press.

2. Sew the Pocket Full of Posies block to the left side of the green Flower Pot block that has only two rows; press. Sew this unit to the bottom of the Birds in My Garden block; press.

3. Sew the units from steps 1 and 2 together; press.

Row 4

Assembling Row 5

1. Sew a cream tone-on-tone 3½" square to the left side of a cream print 3½" square; sew a cream tone-on-tone 3½" x 21½" rectangle to the right side. Refer to the row 5 diagram and sew the remaining row from the Flower Pot block in row 4 to the right side; press.

2. Sew one blue Flower Pot block to each side of one green Flower Pot block as shown. Sew a cream print 3½" x 12½" rectangle to the left side; press. Sew the unit from step 1 to the top edge; press.

3. Sew a Blooming Button Flower block to the left edge; press.

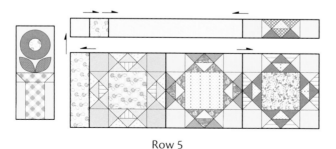

Row 5

Assembling the Quilt Top

1. Sew the rows together in numerical order.

2. Sew two blue checked 1½" x 42" border strips together end to end. Repeat to make a second set. Referring to "Adding Borders" on page 10, use the quilt center as a guide and cut two side borders the length of the quilt. Sew these borders to the sides; press. Sew the remainder of the strips from the side borders to two blue checked 1½" x 42" strips. Using the quilt center as a guide, cut these borders to fit the top and bottom of the quilt. Sew these borders to the top and bottom; press.

3. Repeat step 2 using two yellow floral 5½" strips for the sides and one and one-half yellow floral 5½" strips for the top and bottom; press.

Finishing the Quilt

1. Piece the backing fabric using a horizontal seam.

2. Layer and baste the quilt. Quilt as desired.

3. Referring to "Binding" on page 10 and using the striped 2½"-wide bias strips, attach the binding to your quilt.

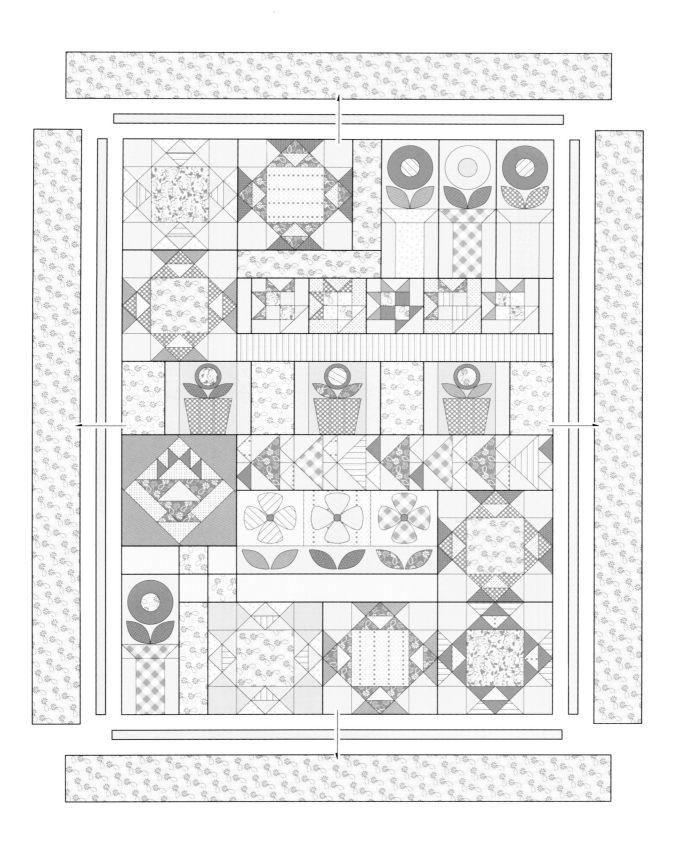

Patterns

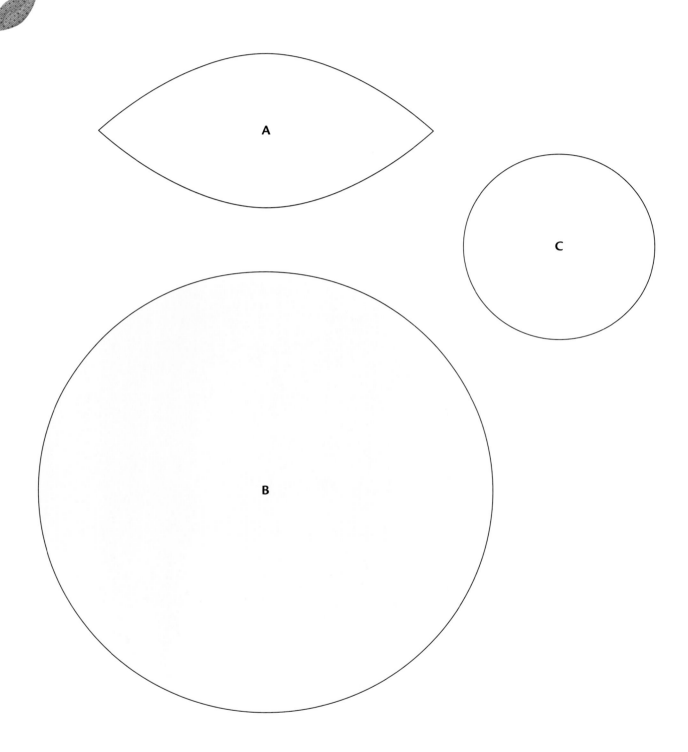

A

C

B

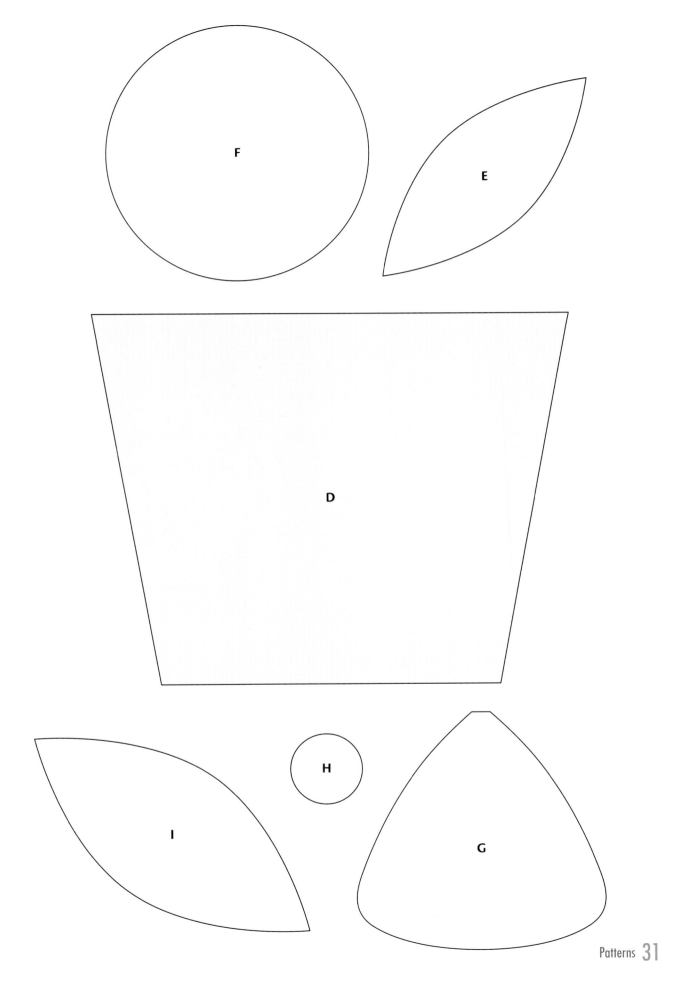

About the Author

Cindy Lammon took her first quilting class in 1981 and was hooked immediately! A love of fabric, pattern, and design has fueled her passion for quilting for over 28 years. She enjoys machine piecing and machine quilting, but she also loves hand quilting and hand appliqué.

Cindy teaches many classes at Raspberry Patch Quilt Shop in Cottleville, Missouri, and lectures for quilt guilds in the Saint Louis area. This is her second book with Martingale & Company.

Cindy has two children and one granddaughter and lives with her husband, Mike, outside of Saint Louis. If she's not sewing, she's busy with quilt guilds, quilt retreats, and playing in the garden!